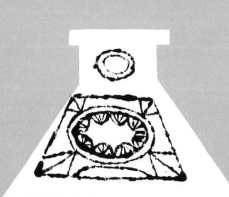

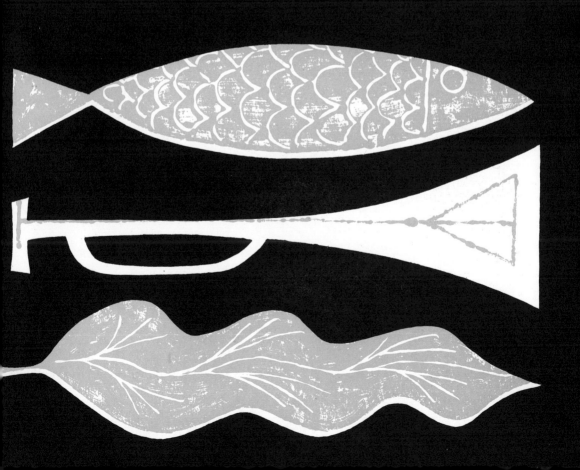

Do You See What I See?

Written and illustrated by

Helen Borten

ABELARD-SCHUMAN

London   New York

An Intext Publisher

ISBN: 0.200.71301.9 Trade
ISBN: 0.200.71845.2 RB

NEW YORK   TORONTO
Abelard-Schuman   *Abelard-Schuman*
Limited   *Canada Limited*
257 Park Ave. S.   *228 Yorkland Blvd.*
10010   *425*

To Peter

I see lines and shapes and colors
everywhere around me.

This is a line. _____

This is a shape.

This is a color.

When you put them together, they make a picture.
Some pictures make me laugh out loud; others make
me want to cry. Some pictures are as exciting
as a ride on a roller coaster. Others make me feel
as quiet as falling snow. That's because the lines
and shapes and colors in them are arranged
in different ways.

Up and down lines pull
me up, up, up with them,
until I feel as tall as
a steeple and as taut as
a stretched rubber band.
I think of lofty things—
giant redwood trees, a
lighthouse rising above
the sea, a rocket soaring
high into the sky, noble
kings in flowing robes.

Flat lines, side by side, make me feel calm and peaceful.
I think of ploughed fields stretching across the countryside.

And I remember
- floating like a log on the smooth surface of a lake.

Slanted lines can rush
me downward on a slide or sliding
pond. Or they can soar me high
on a pair of skis. For slanted lines
are like a seesaw—sometimes
they go up, and sometimes
they come down.

Lines can bend like rows of wheat when a soft breeze blows. They can bend in other ways too. Lines that bend in a zigzag way seem to crackle with excitement. They make me think of thunder storms and jagged mountain peaks. I see the huge jaws of a crocodile, wide open and bristling with jagged teeth, ready to snap shut.

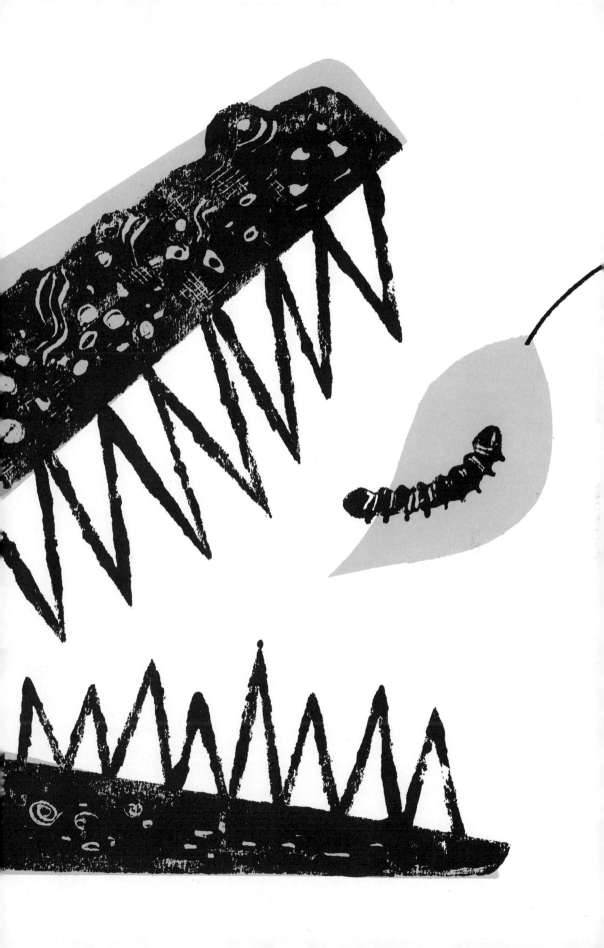

Lines can bend in a curved way, too.
A curved line is like a swan, full of
beauty and grace. It can rise and curl
slowly, as lazy as smoke. It can twirl
like a dancer, or flow and swirl like
water in a stream full of speckled fish.

Lines can be as thin and delicate as a spider web,
or as heavy and black as the bars of a lion's cage.

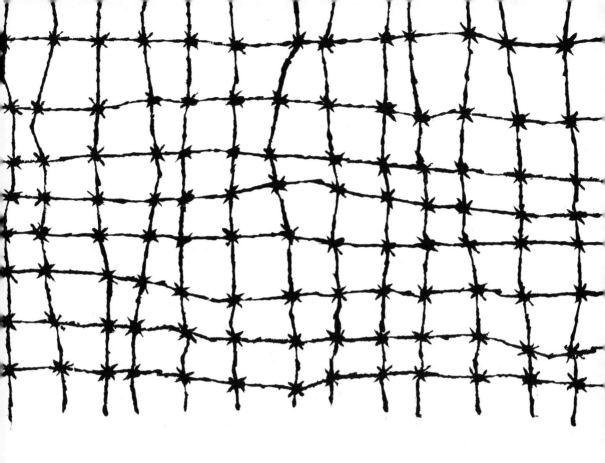

Lines can be as ragged as a barbed wire fence,
or as smooth as the thread in mother's sewing box.

I see lines everywhere around me—
skinny ones and fat ones, timid ones and bold ones,
wiggly ones and straight ones, hard ones and soft ones,
shaggy ones and smooth ones, fast ones and slow ones.

Wherever I look I see lines
making patterns of beauty.
Can you see them, too?

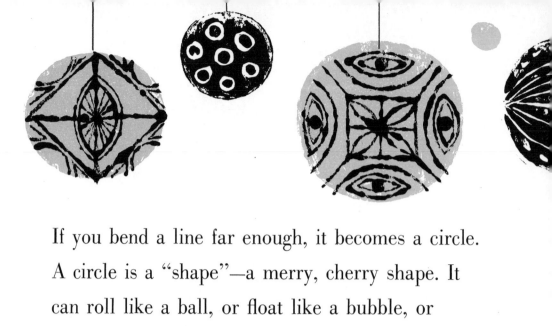

If you bend a line far enough, it becomes a circle.
A circle is a "shape"—a merry, cherry shape. It
can roll like a ball, or float like a bubble, or
turn like a ferris wheel. It can be as calm as the
moon, as gentle as a curled-up kitten, or as fat
and jolly as Santa Claus.

Some circles can even make you giggle!
Have you ever watched a frog about to sing?
He blows his throat up like a balloon and
out comes "chugaroom, chugaroom."

When four straight lines meet like this □ the shape they make is called a "square." Now, a square can never roll like a ball. But it can stand as steady as your building blocks. Squares have a neat, careful look, like a window screen or a checkerboard.

A high building is like a square that has been stretched and stretched until it is tall and skinny. That kind of shape is called a "rectangle." A big city looks like a maze of squares and rectangles piled on top of each other, with little ones inside of big ones.

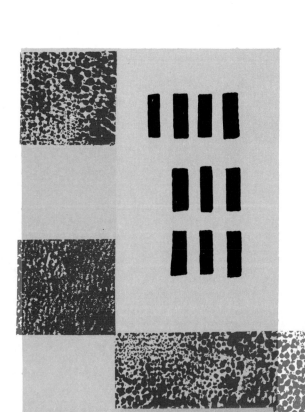

When three straight lines meet like this △
the shape they make is called a
"triangle." It seems to me
that triangles push
and pull in a
hard, stiff
way.

And
sometimes
they force me to
look where they are
pointing, like an arrowhead on a sign.
Here are some things that look like triangles.

One day I saw six jet planes flying by.

They looked like six silver triangles flying in a row.

Did you ever see a sly, red fox?

His pointed face is almost as sharp as a triangle.

I see shapes everywhere around me —
skinny ones and fat ones, smooth ones
and lumpy ones, squeezed-in ones and
pushed-out ones.

You have a shape. And so does your
dog and your toys and the flowers and
butterflies in your garden. You see,
everything in the world has a shape!

Everything has a color, too. Different colors make
us feel different ways, just as lines and shapes do.
Red is hot like a crackling fire,
and blue is cold like a mountain stream.

Yellow is warm like the sun's rays,
and green is as cool as a crisp leaf of lettuce.

Colors can be pale and timid as a mouse —
or dark and mysterious as the night.

Some colors are as dull as the sky on a rainy
day when everything is dripping and gray.
Others are so bright they make me blink.
Bright colors clang for attention like a
fire engine. They are as exciting as city
lights flashing on and off after dark.

Sometimes colors that are next to each other stand
out as clear and bold as the stripes on a zebra.
But sometimes you can hardly tell where one color
stops and another color begins. Way, way out
where the ocean meets the sky is like that.
I see colors everywhere around me — warm ones
and cool ones, bright ones and dull ones, clear
ones and muddy ones, gay ones and sad ones.

I see the world as a great big painting, full of
lines and shapes and colors, to look at and enjoy.
Do you see
What I see?

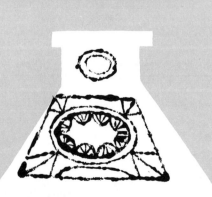

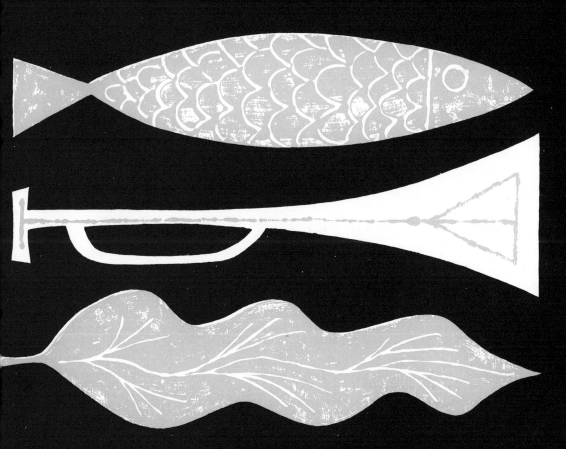